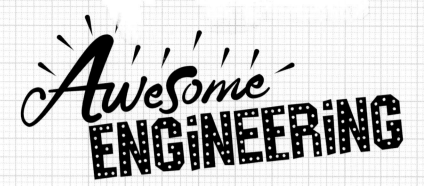

Awesome ENGiNEERiNG

TUNNELS

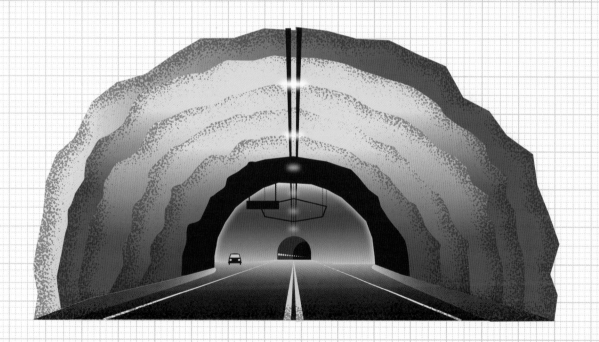

SALLY SPRAY
WITH ARTWORK BY MARK RUFFLE

Franklin Watts

Published in paperback in Great Britain in 2019 by
The Watts Publishing Group
Copyright © The Watts Publishing Group, 2017

Series editor: Paul Rockett
Series design and illustration: Mark Ruffle
www.rufflebrothers.com
Consultant:
Andrew Woodward BEng (Hons) CEng MICE FCIArb

ISBN 978 1 4451 5536 4

Printed in China

Franklin Watts
An imprint of
Hachette Children's Group
Part of The Watts Publishing Group
Carmelite House
50 Victoria Embankment
London EC4Y 0DZ
An Hachette UK Company
www.hachette.co.uk
www.franklinwatts.co.uk

Picture credits: Natalia Bratslavsky/
Dreamstime: 29tl; Agencja Fotograficzna
Caro/Alamy: 27bl; 88studio/Shutterstock:
29tr; Therme Erding/CC Wikimedia
Commons: 28tr; International Newsreel/
Wikimedia Commons: 11t; JPL-Caltech/
NASA: 29tc; Thomas Jurkowski/
Dreamstime: 25cr; LOC/Corbis Historical/
Getty Images: 8bl; Mrak.hr/Shutterstock:
19tr; Cornelia Pithart/Shutterstock: 28tl;
Qaphotos.com/Alamy: 15b; Science
& Society PL/Getty Images: 7cr; Remy
Steinegger/Reuters/Alamy: 27cr;
Wandee007/Shutterstock: 19cr; Captain
Yeo/Shutterstock: 28tc.

MIX
Paper from
responsible sources
FSC® C104740

FSC
www.fsc.org

CONTENTS

4 Can You Dig It?

6 Thames Tunnel

8 New York City Subway

10 Holland Tunnel

12 Seikan Tunnel

14 Channel Tunnel

16 Drogden Tunnel

18 Lærdal Tunnel

20 Boston Big Dig

22 SMART Tunnel

24 Large Hadron Collider

26 Gotthard Base Tunnel

28 Fascinating Facts

30 Further Information

31 Glossary

32 Index

CAN YOU DIG IT?

Tunnels are dug into the landscape, linking places and people through difficult terrain or even underwater.

Tunnel building began around 3,000 years ago as people found ways of building safe underground links. Since then, thanks to ingenious engineering, tunnels have become longer, deeper and more ambitious.

2180–2160 BCE

Brick-lined tunnels in Babylonia were used to move water from place to place.

36 BCE

A tunnel was built connecting Naples to Pozzuoli in Italy. It featured basic ventilation so people didn't run out of air while underground.

1681

The Midi Canal system in France has a tunnel for boats. It was the first tunnel built using gunpowder to blast through rocks.

1825

Marc Isambard Brunel's invention of the tunnelling shield allowed him to dig the first tunnel under a major river in 1843. This was the Thames Tunnel in London, UK (see page 6).

1867

In Sweden, Alfred Nobel invented dynamite to help blast through rocks.

1874

Peter M Barlow and James Henry Greathead combined their design ideas to make a circular tunnelling shield. It was used to build the world's first underground railway – the London Underground.

WORLD'S LONGEST TUNNELS

The world's longest tunnels supply water into towns and cities. Here are the top six:

Delaware Aqueduct, New York, USA: 137 km
Päijänne Water Tunnel, Finland: 120 km
Dahuofang Water Tunnel, Liaoning Province, China: 85.3 km
Orange-Fish River Tunnel, South Africa: 82.8 km
Bolmen Water Tunnel, Sweden: 82 km
Tunnel Emisor Oriente, Mexico: 62.5 km

Follow the tunnel to find its location.

1907

Carl Akeley invented shotcrete, which is concrete blasted onto tunnel walls using compressed air. This removes water which speeds drying, but most importantly allows concrete to be placed without the use of moulds. It was first used in Chicago, USA.

1927

The Holland Tunnel in New York, USA was the first to use mechanised fans to replace the air in the tunnel (see page 10).

1952

James S Robbins invented the tunnel boring machine, or TBM. This amazing machine revolutionised tunnel building.

THAMES TUNNEL

The Thames Tunnel, built between 1825 and 1843, was a truly revolutionary construction. The first tunnel to go below a major river, it was built using some brand-new engineering techniques. When it opened, it was known as the eighth wonder of the world.

BUILDING BRIEF

Build a tunnel between Rotherhithe and Wapping, under the busy River Thames to allow the transport of people and goods by wagon or carriage.

Engineers: Marc Isambard Brunel, Thomas Cochrane and Isambard Kingdom Brunel

Location: Rotherhithe to Wapping, London, UK

The finished tunnel is 406 m long, 11 m wide, 7 m high and runs 23 m below the surface of the water.

ENTRANCE TOWER

Marc Brunel had a clever plan for how to get underground to where tunnelling under the Thames could begin. A 12-m-high, brick circular wall was built on the soft ground a little way back from the riverbank in Rotherhithe. The wall was strengthened at the top and bottom with iron rings connected by iron rods. Soil was gently removed from under the base, and then gravity took over and the whole structure sank into the soil.

After two months the top of the wall had reached ground level. Foundations were then added and part of the circular wall was removed so that tunnelling could begin.

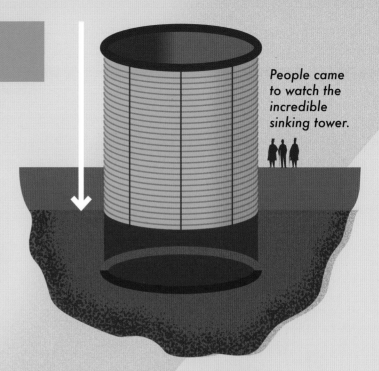

People came to watch the incredible sinking tower.

TUNNELLING SHIELD

Marc Brunel and Thomas Cochrane designed the tunnelling shield, which allowed many workmen to dig the tunnel at the same time.

The large rectangular frame was tall and strong enough to support the roof and sides of the tunnel as it was being built. It had three sections that men could work in, where they used shovels to dig out the soil. The men behind the shield laid the bricks of the tunnel's walls.

The project ran out of money and the ramps for horse-drawn carriages were never built. Instead the tunnel opened for people to walk through. By the end of 1869 it had been adapted for trains and is still used today by busy London commuters.

River Thames

To raise funds for the tunnel, it was turned into a tourist attraction with people paying to see it being built. Big mirrors were put up at the end to make it look longer than it actually was.

NEW YORK CITY SUBWAY

One of the world's largest and busiest underground rail links is the New York City Subway in the USA. It has a vast 1,062 km network of tunnels, and transports nearly six million people around the city every weekday. It first opened in 1904 and has been expanding ever since.

BUILDING BRIEF

Build a rail system for a growing city to provide commuter links that won't disturb the city streets.

Engineer: William Barclay Parsons

Location: New York City, USA

CUT AND COVER

The subway's early tunnels were built using the 'cut and cover' method. Here, huge trenches were dug straight down into the streets. Wooden frames were used to support the ground allowing the brick tunnel to be built. Once the tunnel was built it was then covered over with soil. Digging like this was difficult; traffic was disrupted and sewer, gas and water pipes had to be relocated as the construction progressed.

Tunnels were finished inside with brickwork, creating arches. Concrete and steel bases were laid on the ground for the rails to be placed on.

Harlem River→

Bronx

Hudson River

Manhattan

Central Park

Wooden frames supported the excavation whilst the tunnel was built inside. Street traffic was redirected around the trenches on steel and wooden bridges.

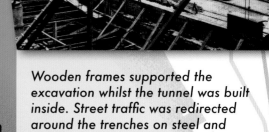

Wooden frame   Soil covering

Brick arches

HARLEM TUNNEL

One of the subway tunnels runs under the Harlem River. When work began in 1913, a trench was dug in the riverbed. Cast iron sections were bolted together to form the four tubes of the tunnel (see below). The tubes were floated out to the river and sunk into the trench by filling them with water. They were surrounded and encased in concrete to keep them in place and stop them floating away when the water was pumped out of them.

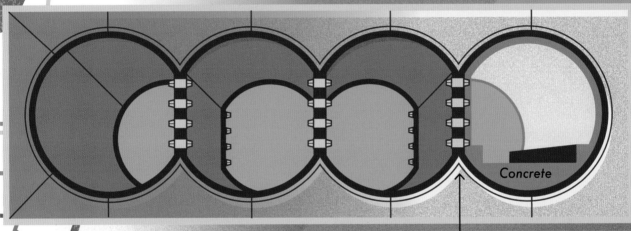

Concrete

Precast steel bolted together

LATER ...

The New York City Subway has continued to grow and expand over the years to keep up with growing demand. The latest development is the 2nd Avenue Expansion, extending tracks from Manhattan to the east side of the city. As tunnelling techniques have moved on, the digging work has been going on right under the streets and subway lines, using massive tunnel boring machines that cut through the rock without anyone noticing above (see page 14).

Brooklyn

HOLLAND TUNNEL

In the 1920s, road traffic was increasing at an astonishing rate in New York City, USA. The solution was the Holland Tunnel. Built under the Hudson River, it linked Manhattan and New Jersey and created a new road link to ease traffic jams in the busy city.

BUILDING BRIEF

Build a tunnel for busy New Yorkers to take the growing number of motor cars in the city across the Hudson River.

Engineer: Clifford Holland and Milton Harvey Freeman, who both died during the project. It was finished by Ole Singstad.

Location: New York City, USA

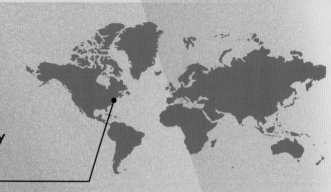

WHY BUILD A TUNNEL?

During the 1920s, ships with tall masts still sailed up the Hudson River. This meant that any bridge across the water would need to be very high, to allow them to travel beneath. But high bridges need a lot of space either end – to allow traffic to travel on and off the bridge – and there wasn't enough room. So a tunnel was thought to be the best solution!

Land ventilation station

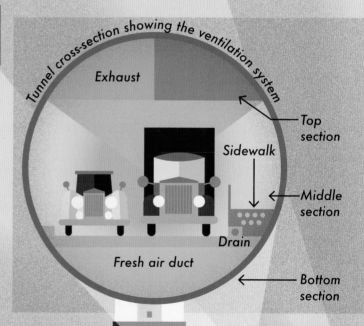

Tunnel cross-section showing the ventilation system

Exhaust

Top section

Sidewalk

Middle section

Drain

Fresh air duct

Bottom section

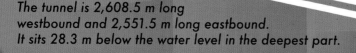

The tunnel is 2,608.5 m long westbound and 2,551.5 m long eastbound. It sits 28.3 m below the water level in the deepest part.

CONSTRUCTION

The twin-tunnel design carries two lanes of traffic going each way. The tunnels had to be dug into the seabed by hand with the men working in caissons – watertight chambers made for digging under rivers. Forty-five men at a time worked in the cramped conditions, digging and blasting their way through the rock on the riverbed. The areas dug out were lined with 70,000 cast-iron supports. To finish the inside walls, 6,000,000 ceramic tiles were laid.

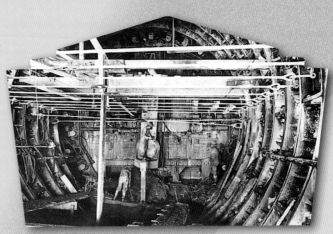

Building the tunnel in 1923

VENTILATION SYSTEM

The tunnel crossing used a revolutionary ventilation system designed by engineer Ole Singstad. He concluded that the round tunnel needed to be divided into three sections. The clean air was blown in through the bottom section, the middle section was where the roadway was laid and the upper section removed the dirty exhaust fumes. There are a total of 84 fans – 42 blow clean air into the tunnels and the other 42 remove the fumes.

The air enters and exits the tunnels though four ventilation stations, positioned along the length of the tunnel – two placed in the river, the other two on the riverbanks. The air in the tunnel is changed completely every 90 seconds. It's thought that the air in the tunnel may be cleaner than on some streets in New York City.

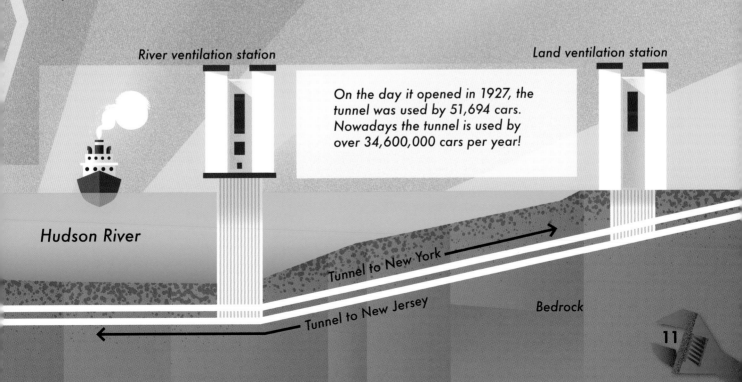

River ventilation station

Land ventilation station

On the day it opened in 1927, the tunnel was used by 51,694 cars. Nowadays the tunnel is used by over 34,600,000 cars per year!

Hudson River

Tunnel to New York

Tunnel to New Jersey

Bedrock

SEIKAN TUNNEL

At 53.85 km, the Seikan Tunnel is the second-longest rail tunnel in the world. Opened in 1988, the tunnel sits 140 m below the seabed and 240 m below sea level. It was built to connect the Japanese islands of Honshu and Hokkaido, replacing a treacherous ferry crossing.

BUILDING BRIEF

Construct a safe route between two of Japan's islands to cope with a growing number of passengers and to increase the movement of trade goods.

Engineer: Japan Railway Construction Corporation

Location: Honshu to Hokkaido, Tsugaru Strait, Japan

DIGGING DOWN

The digging of the tunnel began from both ends. The rock under the seabed would sometimes crack, so driving the tunnels forward was done by drilling through soft rock and blasting harder rock with dynamite. Dug out rubble was removed back through the tunnel by rail. Steel supports were added to the inside of the tunnel to help keep it up, with concrete sprayed over the top to form the inside lining.

HONSHU

The tunnel connects the world's first undersea railway stations: Tappi-Kaitei on Honshu and Yoshioka-Kaitei on Hokkaido.

Tappi-Kaitei Station

In 1983 the tunnels met in the middle with a final blasting of dynamite.

Pilot tunnel — now used as → a collection area for water

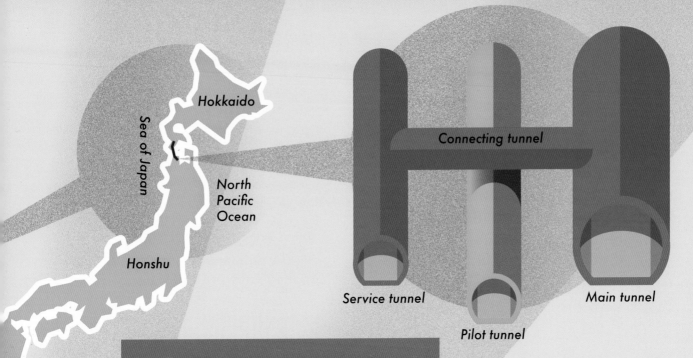

Hokkaido

Sea of Japan

North
Pacific
Ocean

Honshu

Connecting tunnel

Service tunnel

Pilot tunnel

Main tunnel

STOPPING THE LEAKS

When the tunnel digging progressed below the surface of the sea, water began to leak into the tunnel and the battle to keep the inside dry started. In 1976, a 1.5 km section of the tunnel flooded and it took five months to control the flood. From this point, a way of stabilising the rock was developed – holes were bored into the next section of rock to be dug in a fan shape. Grout was pumped into the holes to reinforce the next section to be dug out. This also helped to fill cracks in the rocky seabed where water could come in.

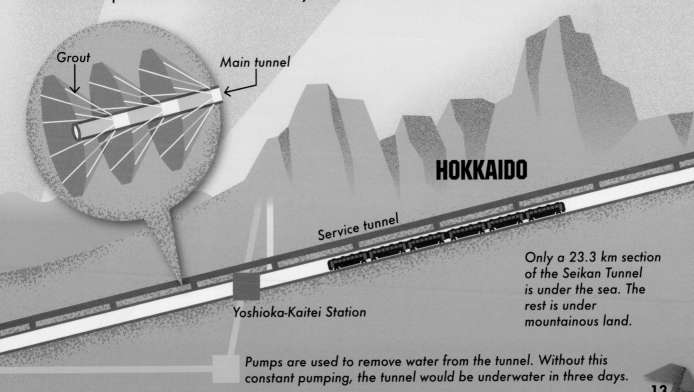

Grout

Main tunnel

HOKKAIDO

Service tunnel

Yoshioka-Kaitei Station

Only a 23.3 km section of the Seikan Tunnel is under the sea. The rest is under mountainous land.

Pumps are used to remove water from the tunnel. Without this constant pumping, the tunnel would be underwater in three days.

CHANNEL TUNNEL

The Channel Tunnel is an engineering wonder – not only does it have the longest undersea section of tunnel in the world, at 37.8 km, but it links two different countries: the UK and France. The idea to build a cross-channel tunnel had been thought of over 200 years ago, but it did not happen until 1988. It took six years to build, with around 13,000 workers.

BUILDING BRIEF

Build a tunnel under the English Channel at the shortest point between the UK and France, making a fast rail journey from London to Paris possible.

Engineering and construction: Balfour Beatty Construction Company

Location: Folkestone, UK and Coquelles, France

TUNNEL BORING MACHINES

Early surveys of the ground under the English Channel found a seam of chalk marl rock that is strong but a material that is easy for tunnel boring machines (TBM) to tackle. This layer of rock dictated the route to be followed. Each TBM is as long as three football pitches!

Behind the cutter, rock and rubble is channelled onto a conveyor belt that loads the material onto railcars to be taken away. But TBMs do more than just nibble through the rock – they drill holes in the tunnel surface and inject grout and bolts ready to add precast supports made of concrete.

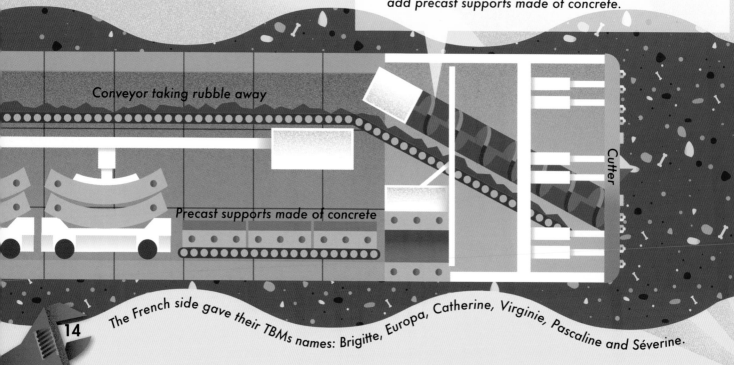

Conveyor taking rubble away

Precast supports made of concrete

Cutter

The French side gave their TBMs names: Brigitte, Europa, Catherine, Virginie, Pascaline and Séverine.

TUNNEL GEOGRAPHY

The Channel Tunnel is actually three tunnels: two larger outside tunnels for carrying the trains in each direction, and one service tunnel in the middle. They are linked every 375 m to allow for an escape route in an emergency. There are also two enormous caverns along the route that allow trains to cross from one line to the other if there is a problem. Each tunnel can be closed off from the other to shut out smoke if there is a fire. A piston relief duct connects the two rail tunnels at the top. This duct allows air to be pushed between the two tunnels as the trains fly by and alter the air pressure.

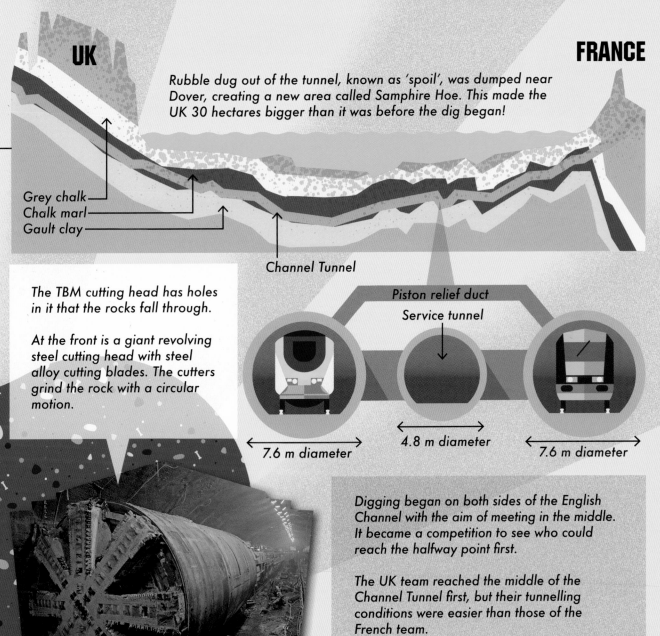

UK

FRANCE

Rubble dug out of the tunnel, known as 'spoil', was dumped near Dover, creating a new area called Samphire Hoe. This made the UK 30 hectares bigger than it was before the dig began!

Grey chalk
Chalk marl
Gault clay

Channel Tunnel

The TBM cutting head has holes in it that the rocks fall through.

At the front is a giant revolving steel cutting head with steel alloy cutting blades. The cutters grind the rock with a circular motion.

Piston relief duct
Service tunnel

7.6 m diameter
4.8 m diameter
7.6 m diameter

Digging began on both sides of the English Channel with the aim of meeting in the middle. It became a competition to see who could reach the halfway point first.

The UK team reached the middle of the Channel Tunnel first, but their tunnelling conditions were easier than those of the French team.

DROGDEN TUNNEL

Did you know that Sweden and Denmark are connected by a bridge that turns into a tunnel? The dazzling engineering combination of the Øresund Bridge and the Drogden Tunnel also includes the artificial island of Perberholm. Together, the three projects form one of the most ambitious engineering projects in the world.

Øresund Bridge

BUILDING BRIEF

Design a link to reach across the 16-km stretch of water between the Swedish city of Malmö and the Danish capital, Copenhagen, to improve trade and tourism. The link must not disrupt shipping in the area or aircraft approaching Copenhagen Airport, and must have minimal environmental impact.

Bridge architect: George K. S. Rotne

Tunnel design and construction: Arup

Location: Malmö, Sweden and Copenhagen, Denmark

THE TUNNEL

It was not possible to dig into the rock under the Drogden Channel, so engineers came up with a plan to sit the tunnel on the seabed. A narrow channel was dug, with dredging diggers loading the spoil material onto barges to be taken away.

Precast concrete sections of the tunnel were manufactured on shore, sealed to make them watertight, and floated out into position. Once above their final positions they were sunk carefully to rest in the trench on the seabed. The tunnel sections were then buried to stop them floating away when the water was pumped out. Once buried, the water was pumped out so the tunnel lining could be completed.

THE BRIDGE

The Øresund Bridge is 7.8 km long and stands 57 m above the water. This height allows for a clear passage for ships passing below. It opened in July 2000 and is the longest combination rail and road bridge in Europe. The railway runs on a lower deck and vehicle traffic on the upper deck.

THE ISLAND

Dredged material from digging the tunnel was used to build up an area in the middle of the channel, which is now the island of Perberholm. This island is where the bridge ends and the tunnel begins. From here onwards, the road and railway run alongside each other.

The island of Perberholm is protected, to attract plants, animals and birds. It is now home to more than 500 different species of plant.

The tunnel has five sections – two for cars, two for trains and one section used for cables, servicing the tunnel and an escape route.

The tunnel is 4 km long and connects to the Danish island of Amager, a suburb of Copenhagen.

Service and escape tunnel

Cable duct

LÆRDAL TUNNEL

At 24.5 km, the Lærdal Tunnel in Norway is the longest road tunnel in the world. It opened in November 2000 and provides a link between two of Norway's major cities. Directing a route underground avoided difficult terrain and left the beautiful Norwegian countryside undisturbed.

BUILDING BRIEF

Design a tunnel to connect the Norwegian cities of Oslo and Bergen, and provide a reliable link across the mountainous region and the many fjords.

Operator: Norwegian Public Roads Administration

Location: Lærdal and Aurland, Norway

DRILLING AND BLASTING

A moveable drilling jumbo machine was used to dig the tunnel by drilling and blasting. It drilled holes into the rock face that were then filled with an explosive to blast the rock away.

A computer worked out the locations to drill and blast and the positions were marked on the rock face with a laser beam. It took 5,000 blasts to clear the whole tunnel. That's 2.5 million kg of explosives!

SCALING AND BOLTING

Creating a tunnel can be a hazardous business. Blasting and removing material can weaken the rock left behind. The force of the rock above needs to settle and redirect its weight around the new tunnel. This can put so much pressure on areas of weak rock that they explode – this is called a 'rock burst'.

To stop rock bursts inside the Lærdal Tunnel it was reinforced using a process called scaling and bolting. Steel bolts were shot into the newly exposed surface, redirecting any weaknesses deeper into the rock. The whole area was then sprayed with shotcrete, a quick-drying liquid concrete reinforced with plastic fibres. It took about 200,000 rock bolts and 45,000 cubic metres of shotcrete to secure the tunnel.

Steel bolts in the rock face

Spraying shotcrete

Drilling jumbo machine

LIGHT SHOW

To keep motorists awake and alert while driving the 20-minute journey underground, the engineers consulted with psychologists and came up with some neat tricks to stop any boredom. Fresh air is provided through the tunnel with fans placed at either end with an air filtration area in the middle. There are three caves along the drive that open out into areas big enough and safe enough to turn around in and to give the driver a break from the white light of the tunnel. The caves are illuminated with blue light, while yellow lights at the edges are designed to look like a sunrise.

BOSTON BIG DIG

By the 1980s, the roads of Boston, USA, were no longer able to cope with the city's increased traffic. The solution was the Big Dig. This was an enormous engineering plan that took 16 years to build, with tunnels to put the main city roads underground, and a tunnel built under Boston Harbour.

Existing road
New road
New tunnel

BUILDING BRIEF

Design and construct a new underground road system for the centre of Boston, USA. It should ease the increasing traffic and provide new links around the city.

Engineers: Bill Reynolds, Frederick P. Salvucci

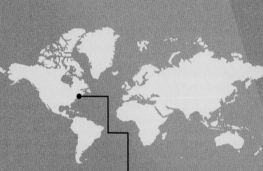

Location: Boston, USA

GROUND FREEZING

Ground-freezing pipe

Some of the ground around Boston is very soft and difficult to excavate, so engineers froze the ground temporarily to stabilise it as they dug. To do this, special pipes were put into the ground and cooled with salt water or liquid nitrogen, turning the water in the surrounding soil to ice.

SLURRY WALLS

Slurry walls made it possible for engineers to tunnel through Boston's soft, water-laden soil. To build a slurry wall:

1. a guide wall is built and a trench dug alongside it;

2. as it is built it is also filled with slurry (a mixture of water and clay). The pressure of the slurry prevents the walls of the trench from collapsing;

3. a steel cage is put into the slurry. Concrete is then pumped into the trench, starting at the bottom. As the concrete is pumped in it pushes the slurry out. Once set, the concrete forms a single panel to the tunnel wall.

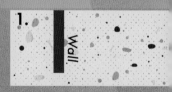

Wall

Slurry

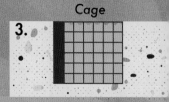

Cage

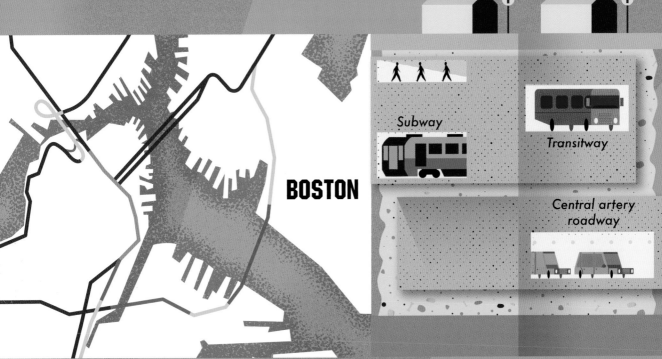

BOSTON

Subway

Transitway

Central artery roadway

Boston road and tunnel map

The Boston Big Dig created lots of different tunnels under the city to accommodate pedestrains, trains, trams and cars.

TUNNEL JACKING

Tunnels had to be built under rail lines that were in constant use. Engineers needed to use a technique called tunnel jacking. This involves pushing a giant, hollow concrete box through the earth – in this case directly under the rail lines. As it is pushed through the earth, the earth is dug out and removed from the box. As the box is moved forward, supports are added to the tunnel space behind.

Push

TED WILLIAMS TUNNEL

The Ted Williams Tunnel was built under Boston Harbour as an extra highway. It is 2.6 km long and made from steel sections covered in concrete. The twin-tubed sections, which looked like giant binoculars, were made off site and floated into place. They were laid in a dredged channel and joined together to form the tunnel. Each tube carries two lanes of traffic. The tunnel is named after a famous Boston Red Sox baseball player, and was opened to all traffic in 2003.

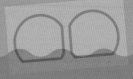

SMART TUNNEL

The SMART Tunnel, in Kuala Lumpur, Malaysia, stands for Stormwater Management And Road Tunnel – and it is a very smart tunnel indeed! It copes with the heavy traffic in the area and also provides a fantastic drainage system in times of flooding. The tunnel opened in 2007.

BUILDING BRIEF

Design and build a tunnel to carry floodwater from the Klang and Gombak rivers away from the centre of the city and add sections for cars.

Engineer: MMC Engineering-Gamuda, Mott MacDonald and SSP Consultants, Gustav Klados (Senior Project Manager)

Location: Kuala Lumpur, Malaysia

DUAL PURPOSE

When designing the stormwater tunnel, engineers decided that it could also be used as a road link. Cars could then travel under the city rather than through it. So the tunnel was built with two road sections and a section at the bottom for floodwater.

Lorries and motorbikes aren't allowed to use the tunnel as they may cause more accidents than cars alone.

The tunnel is 9.7 km in length, of which 4 km is used as a roadway for cars. It is 13.2 m in diameter.

CRACKS AND CAVES

The tunnel was dug with two specially designed TBMs. They started in the middle of the tunnel and dug outwards. The stone in Kuala Lumpur sits on limestone, which can be dotted with caves and caverns.

Geologists bored holes ahead of the TBMs to check for breaks in the stone structure. If a TBM dug into a space under the ground, it could open up a great cavern called a sinkhole. Where cracks, holes and other weaknesses were discovered, a concrete-based grout was pumped in to fill the empty spaces providing a soft and safe ground for the TBM to drill into.

THREE MODES

The completed tunnel operates in three modes:

Mode 1 – when there is little or no rain, the cars can use the two road tiers of the tunnel.

Mode 2 – when there is moderate rain, the two tiers of road are OK for cars to use, but the bottom drainage tier is also used to direct rainwater to a river south of the city.

Mode 3 – about twice a year when there is lots of rain and the city is in danger of flooding, the tunnel is closed to cars and the stormwater is allowed to flow through all three sections of the tunnel.

After the tunnel has been used for floodwater, it is cleaned before cars are allowed to use it again. This takes about two days.

LARGE HADRON COLLIDER

There are a number of ways in which the Large Hadron Collider Tunnel is different from other tunnels. It's not a transport link. It doesn't channel water. And it's completely circular! The tunnel has a circumference of 27 km and is home to the Large Hadron Collider – an instrument that seeks to reproduce the conditions that existed at the time of the Big Bang.

BUILDING BRIEF

Use an existing tunnel to house the Large Hadron Collider.

Construction project engineer: John Osborne at CERN

Location: Geneva, Switzerland

The Large Hadron Collider was built by CERN – the European Council for Nuclear Research – an organisation that was founded in 1954.

THE TUNNEL

The tunnel was excavated between 1985 and 1988 using three TBMs and was originally designed for an earlier machine – the Large Electron-Positron Collider. The tunnel sits an average of 100 m underground. Experiments are easier to control here as they are unaffected by temperature change and radiation from the Sun. The Large Hadron Collider's first experiment took place in 2008.

WHAT THE LARGE HADRON COLLIDER DOES

The Large Hadron Collider is a particle accelerator – the biggest and most powerful in the world. It's a machine that sends two particle beams at almost the speed of light in opposite directions around the tunnel, in the hope that they will collide. Magnets placed around the tunnel make the beams curve. Meanwhile, four particle detectors gather clues about the collision of particles, to help physicists understand more about the beginning of the Universe.

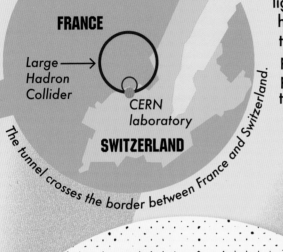

FRANCE

Large → Hadron Collider

CERN laboratory

SWITZERLAND

The tunnel crosses the border between France and Switzerland.

A particle detector

MOON MOVEMENT

Although placing the Hadron Collider underground means that conditions for experiments are easier to control, there is one day of the month when things change. On the nights when there is a full Moon, the Earth's crust rises by about 25 cm. This causes the tunnel edge, or circumference, to stretch by about 1 mm. This is not a big change, but big enough that the physicists have to take it into account as they analyse their test results!

What is dark matter? What is anti-matter? What are black holes? Scientists at CERN hope that the Large Hadron Collider will help them discover the answers to these big questions and many more ...

GOTTHARD BASE TUNNEL

Many tunnels run beneath the mountains of the Alps, but the longest and deepest of them all is the Gotthard Base Tunnel, completed in 2016.

BUILDING BRIEF

Design a rail link to run through the Saint-Gotthard Massif mountain range to provide high-speed rail links through Switzerland.

Engineers: Ernst Basler + Partner, AlpTransit

Location map: Switzerland

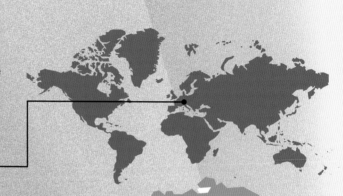

Switzerland

Tunnel route→

DESIGN AND ROUTE

Extensive geological testing had to be carried out to make sure that the mountain rock was stable enough for drilling and could support a tunnel. During the testing a hole was drilled through an area of rock that had water behind it, causing the test tunnel to fill with high-pressure water. This led to the tunnel being redirected to find a deeper route.

Tests showed that the rock much lower down was marble – a hard rock perfect for tunnelling. As a result, it is the deepest rail tunnel in the world, reaching 2.3 km under the ground in some parts.

At 57 km, the Gotthard Base Tunnel is the longest rail tunnel in the world.

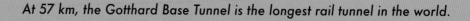

PLAN OF WORKS

To complete the massive dig in time, the tunnelling started in four different places along the route, in Erstfeld, Amsteg, Sedrun and Faido. A further station at the end of the tunnel in Bodio was added later. There were up to 1,000 people working in the tunnel at a time. The project used four gigantic TBMs. The TBMs could tunnel 2 m at a time, digging through the rock, and spraying the uncovered surface with liquid concrete to stabilise the newly dug areas. Work went on for 24 hours a day for six years.

INNER WATERPROOFING

The inner surface of the tunnel is made from concrete. Liquid concrete was added at the first stage to temporarily support the tunnel roof. In some areas where there was ground water, extra material layers were added for waterproofing. First, a layer of plastic mesh, then a layer of plastic sheeting. This keeps all the water in the ground running around the tunnel. A metal mould was then pulled through and normal concrete poured behind to complete the tunnel lining.

Celebrations after the TBM breaks through the rock, completing the tunnel.

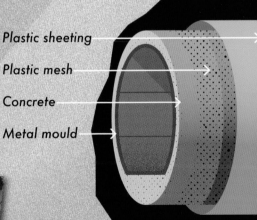

Plastic sheeting

Plastic mesh

Concrete

Metal mould

Spraying concrete onto the tunnel walls of the Sedrun section of the tunnel.

FASCINATING FACTS

Many, many tunnels run under the ground. There might even be a tunnel under your feet right now!

The **Marmaray Tunnel**, opened in 2013, is an immersed tube under the Bosphorus in Istanbul, Turkey. The river splits the city, so one side is in Europe and the other in Asia. The tunnel links these two continents, and it takes just four minutes by train to get from Europe to Asia.

In Shanghai, China, the **Bund Sightseeing Tunnel** takes visitors on a short kaleidoscopic 647-m trip by train through a tunnel of bright lights, sound effects and music.

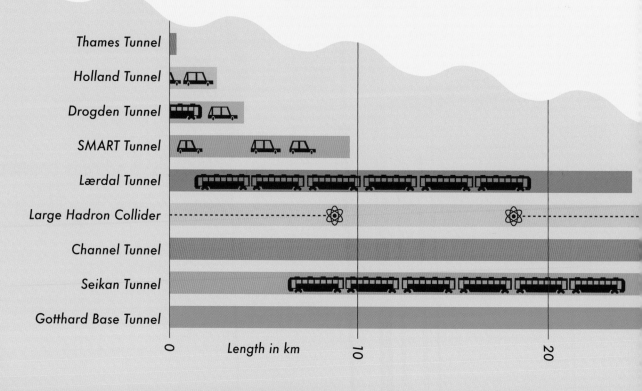

Thames Tunnel

Holland Tunnel

Drogden Tunnel

SMART Tunnel

Lærdal Tunnel

Large Hadron Collider

Channel Tunnel

Seikan Tunnel

Gotthard Base Tunnel

0   Length in km   10   20

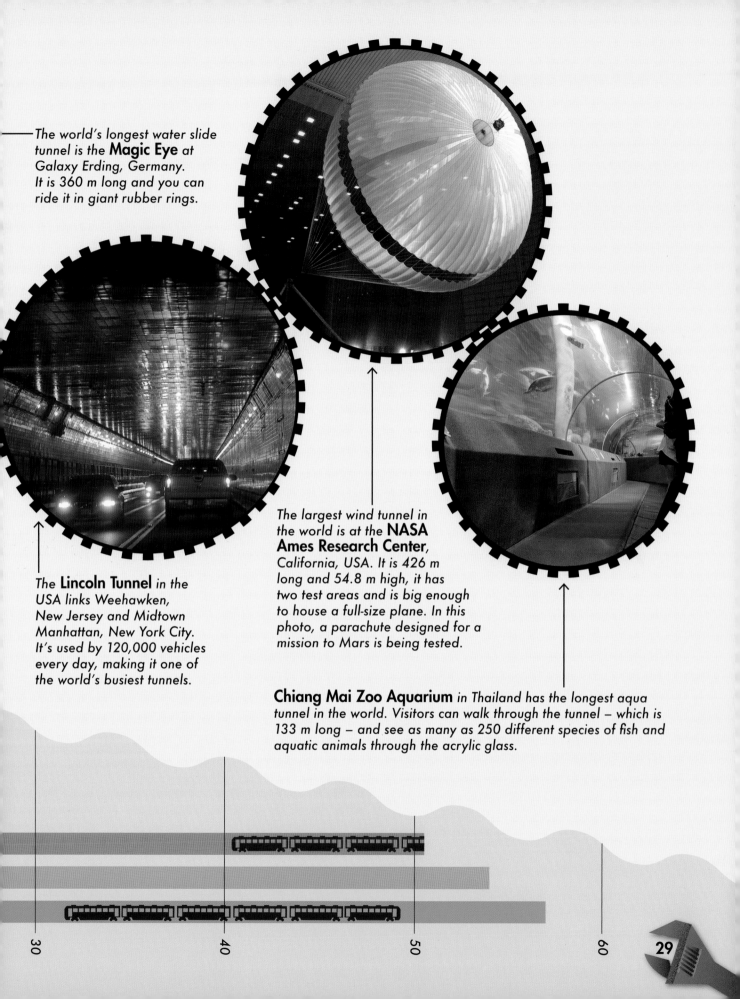

The world's longest water slide tunnel is the **Magic Eye** at Galaxy Erding, Germany. It is 360 m long and you can ride it in giant rubber rings.

The **Lincoln Tunnel** in the USA links Weehawken, New Jersey and Midtown Manhattan, New York City. It's used by 120,000 vehicles every day, making it one of the world's busiest tunnels.

The largest wind tunnel in the world is at the **NASA Ames Research Center**, California, USA. It is 426 m long and 54.8 m high, it has two test areas and is big enough to house a full-size plane. In this photo, a parachute designed for a mission to Mars is being tested.

Chiang Mai Zoo Aquarium in Thailand has the longest aqua tunnel in the world. Visitors can walk through the tunnel – which is 133 m long – and see as many as 250 different species of fish and aquatic animals through the acrylic glass.

30   40   50   60

FURTHER INFORMATION

BOOKS

Amazing Jobs: Engineering by Colin Hyson (Wayland, 2016)

A History of Britain in 12 Feats of Engineering by Paul Rockett (Franklin Watts, 2015)

It'll Never Work: Buildings, Bridges and Tunnels by Jon Richards (Franklin Watts, 2016)

Tremendous Tunnels by Ian Graham (Franklin Watts, 2009)

WEBSITES

A great guide to how tunnels work:
science.howstuffworks.com/engineering/structural/tunnel.htm

Lots of interesting tunnel facts:
www.sciencekids.co.nz/sciencefacts/engineering/tunnels.html

A website full of easy-to-understand science on tunnels:
easyscienceforkids.com/all-about-tunnels/

The BBC Newsround website has information about tunnels, including this link to a history of the London Underground:
www.bbc.co.uk/newsround/46482813

GLOSSARY

acrylic A synthetic (made from chemicals) material that can resemble glass when made into clear sheets.

alloy A substance formed by combing two or more metals.

analyse To study something carefully in order to understand it.

arch A curved structure often used to support the weight of something above it.

Babylonia An ancient empire located in the area of modern-day Iraq.

black hole An area in space where matter has collapsed in on itself, creating an extremely strong gravitational pull.

cast iron An alloy of iron and carbon that is cast in a mould to form hard iron shapes.

cavern A large cave or chamber.

ceramic Clay that has been hardened by heat.

commuter Someone who travels a distance to work.

compressed air Air that has been put under greater pressure than the air in the atmosphere around us.

concrete A liquid material that sets hard, made from stone or gravel, sand and water.

conveyor belt A moving band of fabric, rubber or metal used for transporting objects from one place to another.

dark matter The invisible energy and matter that scientists can't detect but which they believe is out in space.

dredging Removing mud, weeds and rubbish out of a riverbed.

encased Completely surrounded.

engineer A person who designs, constructs and maintains buildings, machines and other structures.

excavation Digging out material from the ground.

fjord A long, narrow, deep inlet of the sea between high cliffs.

foundations The lowest load-bearing part of a building, usually underground.

geologist An expert in rocks and fossils.

gravitational force The strong pulling force of gravity.

gravity The invisible force of attraction between all objects. Earth's gravity keeps our feet on the ground and makes objects fall to the ground.

grout Paste or material used for filling gaps between bricks, slabs and tiles.

immersed Completely submerged in liquid.

ingenious Clever, original and inventive.

kaleidoscopic Optical effect of patterns of light and colours.

landscape An area of land and its features.

laser beam A strong directed beam of light.

limestone A naturally-occurring hard rock often used as a building material.

liquid nitrogen Nitrogen gas cooled to such a low temperature that it becomes a liquid.

mast A tall upright post or pole on a sailing boat.

navigated A planned direct route.

physicist A scientist who is an expert in forces, matter and energy.

piston relief duct In the Channel Tunnel, an air duct that links the two rail tunnels and helps to limit the changes in air pressure as trains pass by allowing some of the high pressure air created by the fast-moving trains to move from one tunnel to the other.

precast An object or material that has already been moulded (cast) into its final shape ready for use.

psychologist An expert in the behaviour and emotions of the human mind.

revolutionary Something that has been changed dramatically.

seam An underground layer of a mineral, such as gold or coal.

service tunnel A tunnel running alongside another tunnel, used for repairs or for emergency vehicles.

sewer An underground pipe used to carry waste water, drainage water or human waste.

shotcrete A mixture of cement, sand and water.

sinkhole An underground hole or cavity, often in limestone, caused by water erosion.

spoil Rubble or waste material removed when digging a tunnel or other building.

stabilising Making something less likely to give way or collapse.

steel A hard, strong metal made by treating iron with heat and mixing carbon with it.

terrain A stretch of land and more particularly its features, such as mountains or valleys.

trench A long narrow ditch.

ventilation The process of putting fresh air into a space.

INDEX

Babylonia 4
Big Bang 24
Boston Big Dig 20–21
Bund Sightseeing Tunnel 28

CERN 24–25
Channel Tunnel 14–15, 28–29
Chiang Mai Zoo Aquarium 29
'cut and cover' building method 8

Drogden Tunnel 16–17, 28–29

engineers/inventors
  Akeley, Carl 5
  AlpTransit 26–27
  Arup 16–17
  Balfour Beatty Construction Company 14–15
  Barlow, Peter M 4
  Basler, Ernst + Partner 26–27
  Brunel, Isambard Kingdom 6–7
  Brunel, Marc Isambard 4, 6–7
  Cochrane, Thomas 6–7
  Freeman, Milton Harvey 10–11
  Greathead, James Henry 4
  Holland, Clifford 10–11
  Japan Railway Construction Corporation 12–13
  Klados, Gustav 22–23
  MMC Engineering-Gamuda 22–23
  Mott MacDonald and SSP Consultants 22–23
  Norwegian Public Roads Administration 18–19
  Osborne, John 24–25
  Parsons, William Barclay 8–9
  Reynolds, Bill 20–21
  Robbins, James S 5
  Rotne, George K. S. 16–17
  Salvucci, P 20–21
  Singstad, Ole 10–11

Gotthard Base Tunnel 26–29

Holland Tunnel 5, 10–11, 28–29

Lærdal Tunnel 18–19, 28–29
Large Hadron Collider Tunnel 24–25, 28–29
Lincoln Tunnel 29
London Underground 4

machine, drilling jumbo 18–19
machine, tunnel boring (TBM) 5, 9, 14–15,
  22–25, 27
Magic Eye 29
Marmaray Tunnel 28
Midi Canal 4

Naples to Pozzuoli tunnel 4
NASA Ames Research Center 29
New York City Subway 8–9
Nobel, Alfred 4

Øresund Bridge 16–17

Perberholm 16–17

Samphire Hoe 15
Seikan Tunnel 12–13, 28–29
shield, circular tunnelling 4, 6–7
shotcrete 5, 19
SMART Tunnel 22–23, 28–29

Ted Williams Tunnel 21
Thames Tunnel 4, 6–7, 28–29
tunnels, water 5

ventilation 4–5, 10–11, 15, 19